Just Because I Am

A Child's Book of Affirmation

Just Because I Am

A Child's Book of Affirmation

By
Lauren Murphy Payne, M.S.W.

Illustrations by Claudia Rohling

Free Spirit ®
PUBLISHING

Minneapolis, Minnesota

Printed in Singapore

Library of Congress Cataloging-in-Publication Data
Payne, Lauren Murphy, 1956–
Just because I am : a child's book of affirmation / by Lauren Murphy Payne : illustrations by Claudia Rohling
     p.   cm.
ISBN 0-915793-60-1
1. Self-perception—Juvenile literature. 2. Self-acceptance—Juvenile literature. 3. Affirmations—Juvenile literature. 4. Self-talk in children. [1. Self-perception. 2. Self-acceptance.]
I. Rohling, Claudia, 1947–   ill. II. Title.
BF697.5.S43P38 1994
305.23'1—dc20
                                                          93-30609
                                                            CIP
                                                            AC

Edited by Pamela Espeland
Book design and production by MacLean & Tuminelly
Color separations, printing, and binding by Tien Wah Press, Singapore.

The illustrations are done in pen and marker on vellum paper.
The type is set in ITC Leawood Medium, composed by MacLean & Tuminelly.

10 9 8 7 6

Free Spirit Publishing Inc.
400 First Avenue North, Suite 616
Minneapolis, Minnesota 55401
U.S.A.
(612) 338-2068

Printed in Singapore

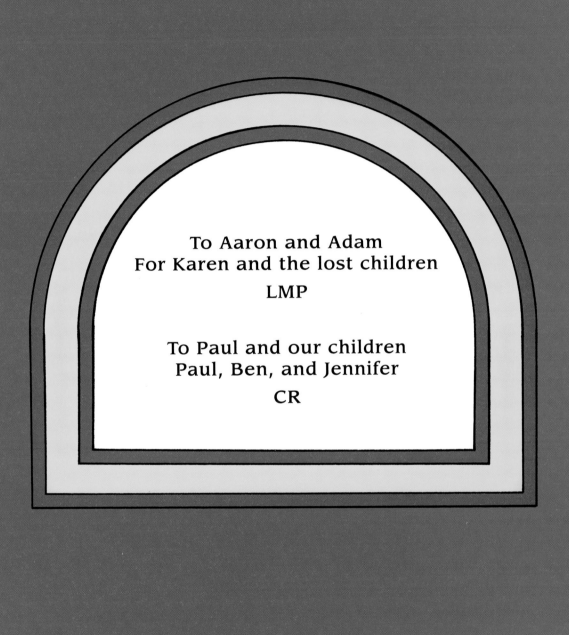

To Aaron and Adam
For Karen and the lost children

LMP

To Paul and our children
Paul, Ben, and Jennifer

CR

I am a person.

I am special.

I am important.

Not because of things I do,

Not because of what
     I look like,

Not because of what
     I have...

Just because I am.

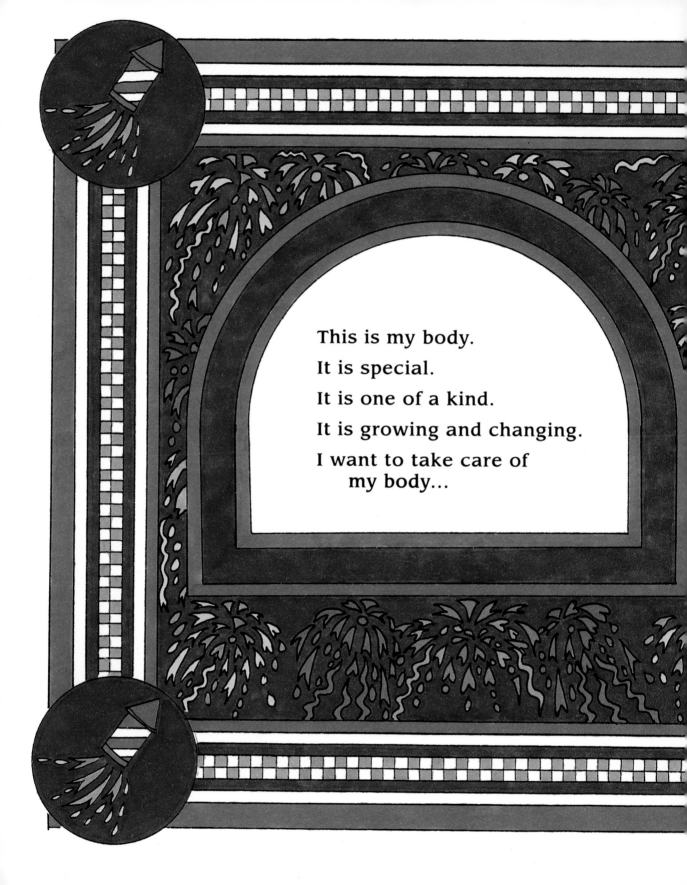

This is my body.

It is special.

It is one of a kind.

It is growing and changing.

I want to take care of
my body...

Because it's mine.

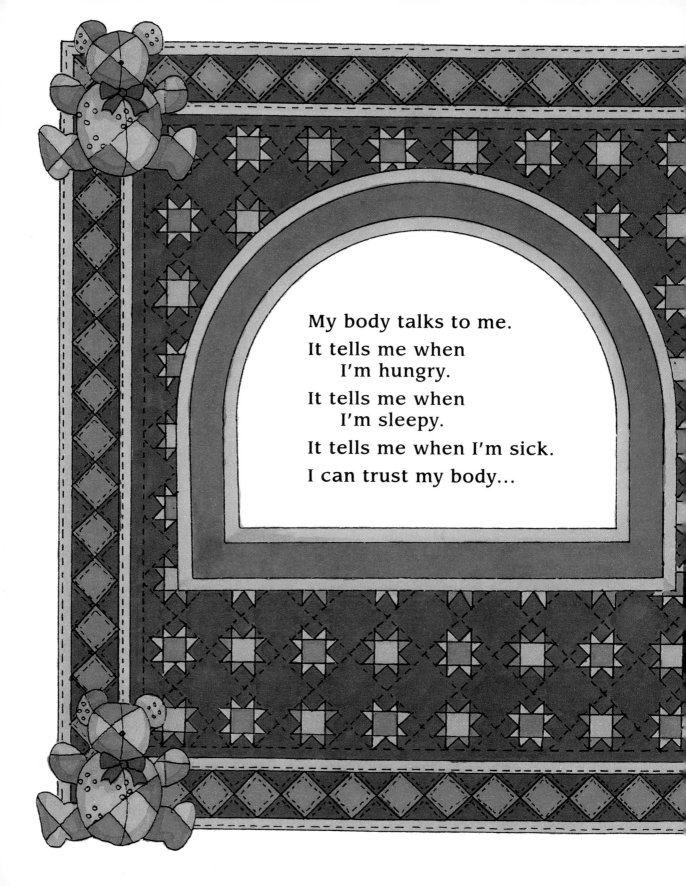

My body talks to me.
It tells me when
    I'm hungry.
It tells me when
    I'm sleepy.
It tells me when I'm sick.
I can trust my body...

To tell me what I need.

Sometimes I have
strong feelings.

I feel anger.

I feel sadness.

I feel fear.

I feel love...

These feelings belong to me.

When I feel angry,

Sometimes I yell.

Sometimes I cry.

Sometimes I talk
to someone I love...

And then I feel better.

When I feel sad,

I need to cry.

I need a hug.

I need to tell someone
about my sadness...

So I know it's okay to be sad.

When I feel scared,

Scared of the dark,

Scared of people and
things I don't know,

I need to feel protected
by someone I trust...

I need to feel safe.

When I feel love,

I feel warm and snuggly.

I feel happy and safe.

I feel important
and special...

I can love myself.

I am learning and
growing every day.

I learn by looking.

I learn by listening.

I learn by doing.

Sometimes I make
mistakes...

That's part of learning, too.

I can make decisions.
Sometimes I say "yes."
I say "yes" to playing
and dancing.
I say "yes" to laughing
and singing.
I say "yes" to hugging
and touching...

When it feels right to me.

STOP

STOP

Sometimes I say "no."

I say "no" to danger.

I say "no" to hugging and touching that feels wrong to me.

I say "no" to strangers and things that hurt me...

I can decide. It's up to me.

I have needs.

It's important to let people know what I need.

I can ask for help when I need it.

I can ask someone who cares about me to help...

And then I know I'm not alone.

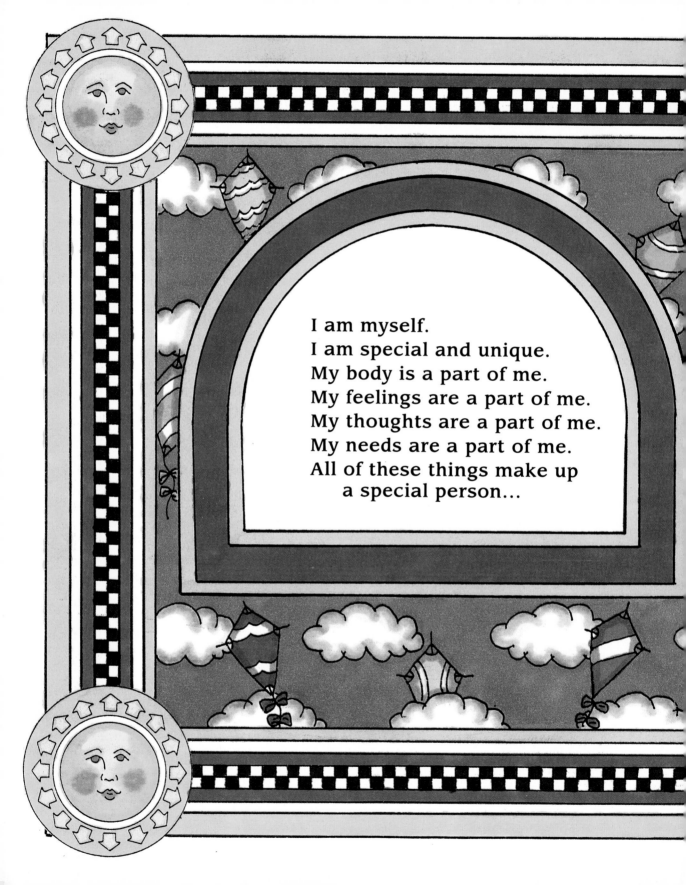

I am myself.
I am special and unique.
My body is a part of me.
My feelings are a part of me.
My thoughts are a part of me.
My needs are a part of me.
All of these things make up
a special person...

Me.

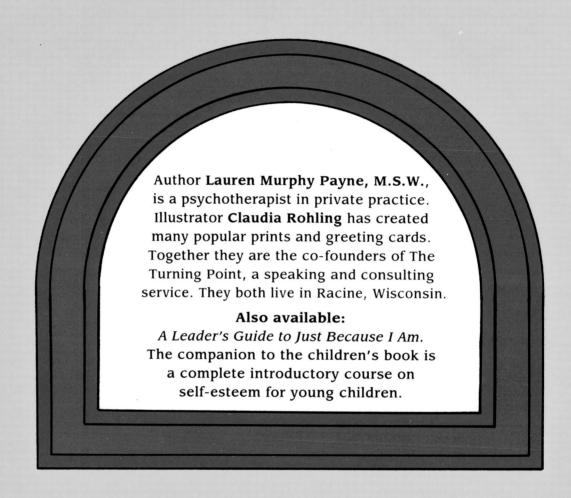

Author **Lauren Murphy Payne, M.S.W.**, is a psychotherapist in private practice. Illustrator **Claudia Rohling** has created many popular prints and greeting cards. Together they are the co-founders of The Turning Point, a speaking and consulting service. They both live in Racine, Wisconsin.

Also available:
A Leader's Guide to Just Because I Am.
The companion to the children's book is a complete introductory course on self-esteem for young children.

To order or request a free catalog, please write or call:

Free Spirit Publishing Inc.
400 First Avenue North, Suite 616
Minneapolis, MN 55401-1730
(800) 735-7323
(612) 338-2068